What Can You Do With Just One Dollar?

By Teresa Vasilopoulos
Illustrated by
Vic Guiza

I COULD USE $3 TO BUY WHATEVER I WANT

BUT WITH $1 I SHOULD DO THE WORLD SOME GOOD

BUT I WONDERED – WHAT GOOD COULD I DO WITH JUST ONE DOLLAR?

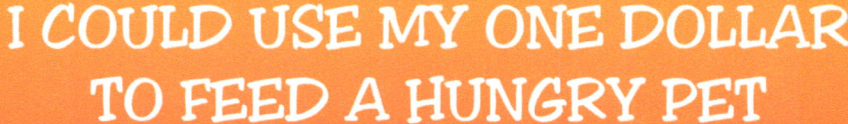

I COULD USE MY ONE DOLLAR TO FEED A HUNGRY PET

OR TO GIVE AWAY KIDS' BOOKS FOR FREE

OR TEACH PEOPLE NOT TO TAKE WATER FOR GRANTED

OR TO HELP A SICK CHILD
BY GRANTING THEIR WISH

OR TO GROW HEALTHY FOOD FOR OTHERS FROM SEEDS

I NEVER KNEW GIVING SOMETHING SO SMALL

COULD MAKE ME FEEL
SO HAPPY AND TALL

WE COULD USE OUR DOLLARS TO BUY POSTERS AND MARKERS

THEN CREATE SIGNS FOR PEACEFUL PROTESTS AND MARCHES

SO TOGETHER WE COULD TRIPLE THE AID!

BY WORKING TOGETHER WE CAN HELP BIG AND SMALL

BY COMBINING OUR DOLLARS WE ALL CAN STAND TALL

EACH NIGHT I DREAM OF WHAT MY DOLLAR CAN DO

HELP JACK JUPITER FEED A STRAY PET!

START

FINISH

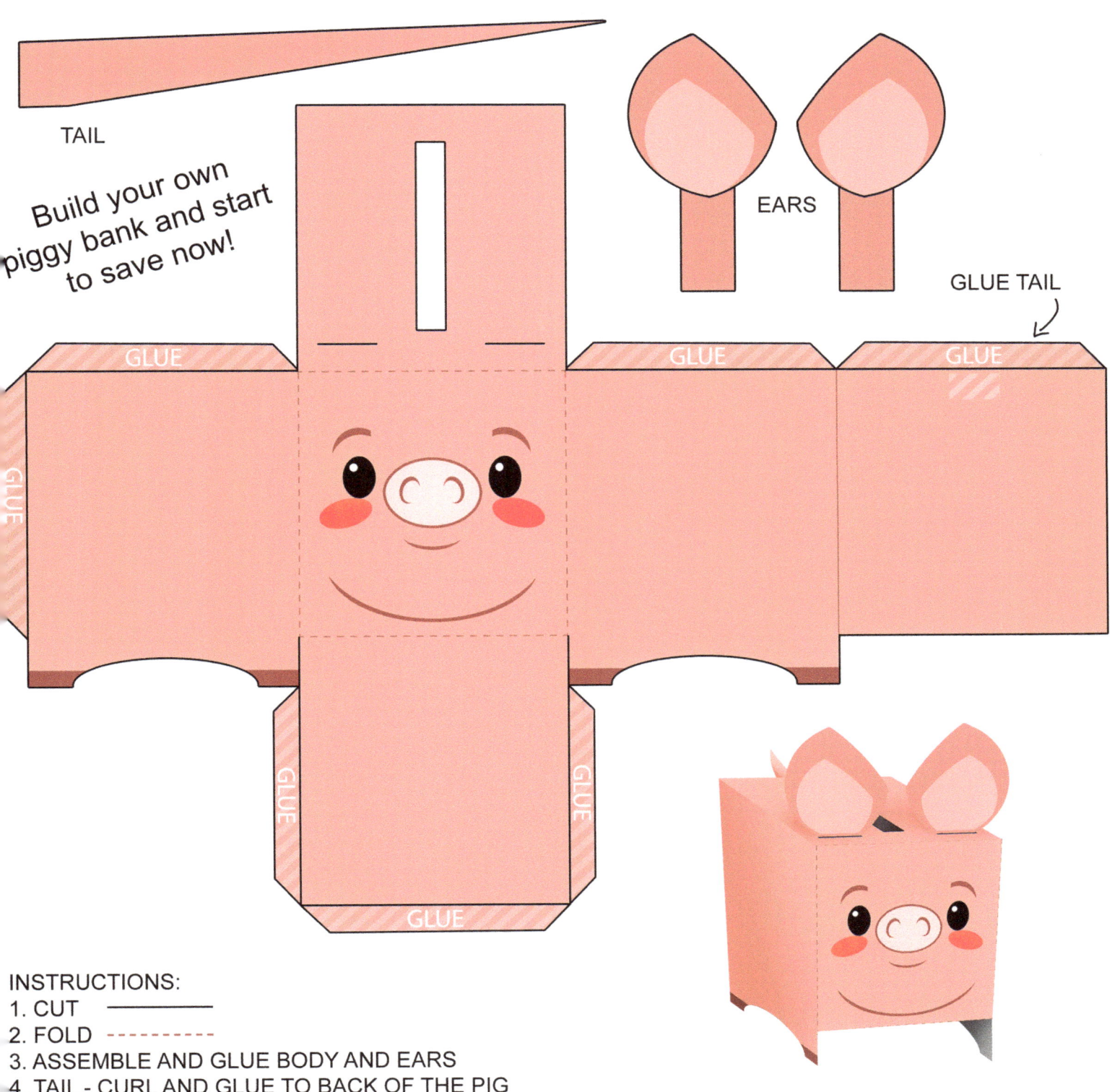

CPSIA information can be obtained
at www.ICGtesting.com
Printed in the USA
BVHW020849190622
640033BV00004B/7